This Planner Belongs To:

_____
_____
_____

**This planner is <u>NOT</u> a legal document and does <u>NOT</u> replace a valid will.

Visit amazon.com/author/donaldedavis for end of life planning workbooks and more.

Copyright© 2019, all rights reserved. Copyright and other intellectual property laws protect these materials. Reproduction or retransmission of the materials, in whole or in part, in any manner, without the prior written consent of the copyright holder, is a violation of copyright law.

Printed in the USA

Table of Contents

Introduction	ii
Personal Information	1
Information About Work/Business	2
My Military Service	3
My Children	4
Who to Call	9
Attorney	9
Doctors	9
Friends and Family	12
Documents You Will Need & Location	22
My Will is Located	22
My Living Will is Located	22
The Family Trust is Located	22
My Power Attorney is Located	22
My Advanced Directive is Located	23
My Health Care Power of Attorney is Located	23
Other Documents are Located	23

Table of Contents

Wishes in Case I Can't Make Decisions	24
Financial Information	25
Bank Accounts	25
Safe Deposit Box	30
Financial Planner	31
Pension and Retirement Accounts	31
Stocks, Bonds, and Mutual Funds	34
Annuities	36
Real Estate Owned	37
Storage Rental	42
Wishes for My Pets	43
Insurance Information	45
Life Insurance	45
Home Insurance	48
Auto Insurance	51
Health Insurance	54
Other Insurances	57

Table of Contents

Household Information	60
Utilities	60
Creditors	61
Subscription Services	62
Social Circle	65
Memberships and Charities	65
Social Information	67
Social Networking Sites	67
My Idea of Final Arrangements	69
Note to Those Left Behind	71
Regrets and Things That Have Bugged Me	74
Proudest Moments	76
Lessons Learned	80
Apologies	83
Aspirations for Others	87
Choices for My Last Days	91
Facts You May Have Not Known	92
Notes and Updates	93

Introduction

FACT: It's unfortunate but true, we all must die one day.

QUESTION: Have you planned for this inevitable and GUARANTEED scenario?

The sad truth is, thousands of people die (whether expected or unexpectedly) each year without the proper end of life planning in place.

Because we all know you love and care about your family and their happiness, one of the best ways you can show this love is by taking time out to document your end of life plan.

Please ask yourself this question: "Today, does my current plans include the message and memory I want to leave behind?" If not, rest assured that your loved ones will be grateful to you for taking this all-important first step!

With this End of Life Planning Workbook you will relieve your loved ones of the added burden of locating your important documents that they will need in order to settle your affairs.

If you own pets, there is space to record what your wishes are for their care. Aspirations for those that you would like to wish the best future. Also, I have included space for you to include any apologies to people that may feel harmed.

Putting directions in writing removes any guesswork and ensures that your final wishes will be met.

Introduction

To be clear, you are free to fill out as much information in this planner as you like or to leave out anything you do not feel applies to you. The more information you leave for your loved ones the easier it will be for them.

Imagine the tremendous sense of accomplishment and peace of mind, you will feel knowing that you:

1. Worked hard and sacrificed the time and effort to take care of your loved ones.
2. You cared enough to plan and prepare for something you knew would be very difficult some day.
3. One of the last memories you will leave behind is showing how much you loved and cared.
4. By minimizing or eliminating many of these emotional and financial pressures, this allows your loved ones to focus on planning your special memorial service and end of life celebration, reflecting on your life's story, and cherish all your great memories shared together.

Wishing you a long and prosperous life,

Donald E. Davis

P.S. Be sure to keep this workbook in a safe place. You could store it in your safe at home or even at your lawyer's office.

Before using a bank safe deposit box consider state and local probate law. Many laws require that a bank safe deposit box be automatically sealed upon your death. This can result in messy complications.

Personal Information

Name:

Maiden Name (*if applicable*):

Address:

Birth Date:

Place of Birth (*include name of hospital, city, county, state, country*):

Citizenship:

My Social Security Number is:

My Birth Certificate/Adoption Record is Located:

My Marriage Certificate is Located:

Personal Information

My Divorce Records/Documents are Located:

My Drivers License is Located:

My Passport is Located:

Information About Work/Business:

Company Name:

Contact Person:

Address:

Phone Number:

Email Address:

Personal Information

Information About Work/Business:

Company Name:

Contact Person:

Address:

Phone Number:

Email Address:

My Military Service:

My Military ID Number is:

Branch of Service:

Years of Service:

Rank at Separation:

Record of Service is Located (DD 214):

My Children

Name

Address:

Phone Number:

Email Address:

Name

Address:

Phone Number:

Email Address:

Notes:

My Children

Name

Address:

Phone Number:

Email Address:

Name

Address:

Phone Number:

Email Address:

Notes:

My Children

Name

Address:

Phone Number:

Email Address:

Name

Address:

Phone Number:

Email Address:

Notes:

My Children

Name

Address:

Phone Number:

Email Address:

Name

Address:

Phone Number:

Email Address:

Notes:

My Children

Name

Address:

Phone Number:

Email Address:

Name

Address:

Phone Number:

Email Address:

Notes:

Who to Call

Attorney:

Name:

Address:

Phone:

Email:

Pastor:

Name:

Address:

Phone Number:

Email Address:

Notes:

Who to Call

Doctors:

Name:

Type of Doctor:

Address:

Phone Number:

Email Address:

Name:

Type of Doctor:

Address:

Phone Number:

Email Address:

Who to Call

Doctors:

Name:

Type of Doctor:

Address:

Phone Number:

Email Address:

Name:

Type of Doctor:

Address:

Phone Number:

Email Address:

Who to Call

Friends & Family:

Name:

Address:

Phone Number:

Email Address:

Name:

Address:

Phone Number:

Email Address:

Notes:

Who to Call

Friends & Family:

Name:

Address:

Phone Number:

Email Address:

Name:

Address:

Phone Number:

Email Address:

Notes:

Who to Call

Friends & Family:

Name:

Address:

Phone Number:

Email Address:

Name:

Address:

Phone Number:

Email Address:

Notes:

Who to Call

Friends & Family:

Name:

Address:

Phone Number:

Email Address:

Name:

Address:

Phone Number:

Email Address:

Notes:

Documents You Will Need & Location

My Will is Located:
___
___
___

My Living Will is Located:
___
___
___

The Family Trust is Located:
___
___
___

My Power of Attorney is Located:
___
___
___

Documents You Will Need & Location

My Advanced Directive is Located:

My Health Care Power of Attorney is Located:

Other Documents are Located (*describe what it is & its location*):

Wishes in Case I Can't Make Decisions

Financial Information

Bank Accounts

Bank:

Address:

Phone:

Checking or Savings:

Name(s) on Account:

Account Number:

Location of Checkbooks, Statements, & Other Info:

Financial Information

Bank Accounts

Bank:

Address:

Phone:

Checking or Savings:

Name(s) on Account:

Account Number:

Location of Checkbooks, Statements, & Other Info:

Financial Information

Bank Accounts

Bank:

Address:

Phone:

Checking or Savings:

Name(s) on Account:

Account Number:

Location of Checkbooks, Statements, & Other Info:

Financial Information

Bank Accounts

Bank:

Address:

Phone:

Checking or Savings:

Name(s) on Account:

Account Number:

Location of Checkbooks, Statements, & Other Info:

Financial Information

Bank Accounts

Bank:

Address:

Phone:

Checking or Savings:

Name(s) on Account:

Account Number:

Location of Checkbooks, Statements, & Other Info:

Financial Information

Safe Deposit Box

Bank:

Address:

Phone:

Box Number:

Location of Key:

Contents:

Financial Information

Financial Planner

Name:

Address:

Phone:

Email Address:

Pension or Retirement Accounts

Type of Account:

Account Number:

Name(s) on Account:

Company:

Address:

Phone:

Financial Information

Pension or Retirement Accounts

Type of Account:

Account Number:

Name(s) on Account:

Company:

Address:

Phone:

Type of Account:

Account Number:

Name(s) on Account:

Company:

Address:

Phone:

Financial Information

Pension or Retirement Accounts

Type of Account:

Account Number:

Name(s) on Account:

Company:

Address:

Phone:

Type of Account:

Account Number:

Name(s) on Account:

Company:

Address:

Phone:

Financial Information

Stocks, Bonds, and Mutual Funds

Type of Account:

Account Number:

Name(s) on Account:

Company:

Address:

Phone:

Type of Account:

Account Number:

Name(s) on Account:

Company:

Address:

Phone:

Financial Information

Stocks, Bonds, and Mutual Funds

Type of Account:

Account Number:

Name(s) on Account:

Company:

Address:

Phone:

Type of Account:

Account Number:

Name(s) on Account:

Company:

Address:

Phone:

Financial Information

Annuities

Annuity Company:

Address:

Phone:

Annuity Owner:

Annuity Number:

Annuity Company:

Address:

Phone:

Annuity Owner:

Annuity Number:

Financial Information

Real Estate Owned

Type of Property (*house, apartment, office, timeshare, other*):

Name(s) on Title:

Address:

Location of Deed:

Value:

Mortgage Company:

Account Number:

Phone:

Financial Information

Real Estate Owned

Type of Property (*house, apartment, office, timeshare, other*):

Name(s) on Title:

Address:

Location of Deed:

Value:

Mortgage Company:

Account Number:

Phone:

Financial Information

Real Estate Owned

Type of Property (*house, apartment, office, timeshare, other*):

Name(s) on Title:

Address:

Location of Deed:

Value:

Mortgage Company:

Account Number:

Phone:

Financial Information

Real Estate Owned

Type of Property (*house, apartment, office, timeshare, other*):

Name(s) on Title:

Address:

Location of Deed:

Value:

Mortgage Company:

Account Number:

Phone:

Financial Information

Real Estate Owned

Type of Property (*house, apartment, office, timeshare, other*):

Name(s) on Title:

Address:

Location of Deed:

Value:

Mortgage Company:

Account Number:

Phone:

Financial Information

Storage Rental

Company:

Address:

Phone:

Unit Number:

Location of Keys:

Access Code:

Contents:

Wishes for My Pets

Wishes for My Pets

Insurance Information

Location of Policies:

Life Insurance

Agent:

Phone:

Email:

Insurance Company:

Address:

Phone:

Policy Owner:

Policy Number:

Insurance Information

Location of Policies:

Life Insurance

Agent:

Phone:

Email:

Insurance Company:

Address:

Phone:

Policy Owner:

Policy Number:

Insurance Information

Location of Policies:

Life Insurance

Agent:

Phone:

Email:

Insurance Company:

Address:

Phone:

Policy Owner:

Policy Number:

Insurance Information

Location of Policies:

Home Insurance

Agent:

Phone:

Email:

Insurance Company:

Address:

Phone:

Policy Owner:

Policy Number:

Insurance Information

Location of Policies:

Home Insurance

Agent:

Phone:

Email:

Insurance Company:

Address:

Phone:

Policy Owner:

Policy Number:

Insurance Information

Location of Policies:

Home Insurance

Agent:

Phone:

Email:

Insurance Company:

Address:

Phone:

Policy Owner:

Policy Number:

Insurance Information

Location of Policies:

Auto Insurance

Agent:

Phone:

Email:

Insurance Company:

Address:

Phone:

Policy Owner:

Policy Number:

Insurance Information

Location of Policies:

Auto Insurance

Agent:

Phone:

Email:

Insurance Company:

Address:

Phone:

Policy Owner:

Policy Number:

Insurance Information

Location of Policies:

Auto Insurance

Agent:

Phone:

Email:

Insurance Company:

Address:

Phone:

Policy Owner:

Policy Number:

Insurance Information

Location of Policies:

Health Insurance

Agent:

Phone:

Email:

Insurance Company:

Address:

Phone:

Policy Owner:

Policy Number:

Insurance Information

Location of Policies:

Health Insurance

Agent:

Phone:

Email:

Insurance Company:

Address:

Phone:

Policy Owner:

Policy Number:

Insurance Information

Location of Policies:

Health Insurance

Agent:

Phone:

Email:

Insurance Company:

Address:

Phone:

Policy Owner:

Policy Number:

Insurance Information

Location of Policies:

Other Insurance (*renter's, pet, motorcycle, etc.*)

Type of Insurance:

Agent:

Phone:

Email:

Insurance Company:

Address:

Phone:

Policy Owner:

Policy Number:

Insurance Information

Location of Policies:

Other Insurance (*renter's, pet, motorcycle, etc.*)

Type of Insurance:

Agent:

Phone:

Email:

Insurance Company:

Address:

Phone:

Policy Owner:

Policy Number:

Insurance Information

Location of Policies:

Other Insurance (*renter's, pet, motorcycle, etc.*)

Type of Insurance:

Agent:

Phone:

Email:

Insurance Company:

Address:

Phone:

Policy Owner:

Policy Number:

Household Information

Utilities

Electricity Company:

Phone:

Account Number:

Water & Gas Company:

Phone:

Account Number:

Telephone Company (*landline*):

Phone:

Account Number:

Telephone Company (*cellular*):

Phone:

Account Number:

Household Information

Creditors

Company:

Phone:

Account Number:

Company:

Phone:

Account Number:

Company:

Phone:

Account Number:

Company:

Phone:

Account Number:

Household Information

Creditors

Company:

Phone:

Account Number:

Company:

Phone:

Account Number:

Company:

Phone:

Account Number:

Company:

Phone:

Account Number:

Household Information

Creditors

Company:

Phone:

Account Number:

Company:

Phone:

Account Number:

Company:

Phone:

Account Number:

Company:

Phone:

Account Number:

Household Information

Subscription Services

Internet Company:

Phone:

Account Number:

Cable Company:

Phone:

Account Number:

Other:

Phone:

Account Number:

Other:

Phone:

Account Number:

Social Circle

Memberships & Charities

Organization:

Address:

Phone:

Membership ID:

Organization:

Address:

Phone:

Membership ID:

Social Circle

Memberships & Charities

Organization:

Address:

Phone:

Membership ID:

Organization:

Address:

Phone:

Membership ID:

Social Information

Social Networking Sites

Facebook:

Login Name:

Password:

Twitter:

Login Name:

Password:

Pinterest:

Login Name:

Password:

LinkedIn:

Login Name:

Password:

Social Information

Social Networking Sites

Other:

Login Name:

Password:

Other:

Login Name:

Password:

Other:

Login Name:

Password:

Other:

Login Name:

Password:

My Idea of Final Arrangements

My Idea of Final Arrangements

Note to Those Left Behind

Note to Those Left Behind

Note to Those Left Behind

Regrets & Things That Have Bugged Me

Regrets & Things That Have Bugged Me

Proudest Moments

Proudest Moments

Proudest Moments

Proudest Moments

Life Lessons Learned

Life Lessons Learned

Life Lessons Learned

Apologies

Apologies

Apologies

Apologies

Aspirations for Others

Aspirations for Others

Aspirations for Others

Aspirations for Others

Choices for My Last Days

Where I Want to Stay:

Company or Alone?

Clergy Visit? Who?

Music Type/Songs?

Facts You May Not Have Known

Favorite Movie(s)

Favorite Actress(es):

Favorite Actor(s):

Favorite Book(s):

Favorite Author(s):

Notes & Updates

Notes & Updates

Notes & Updates

Made in the USA
Middletown, DE
20 July 2023